Further praise fo

An NPR Best Book o...
A *Library Journal* Best Poetry Book of 2021
An NBC News Notable Latino Book of 2021

"For decades . . . [Martín] Espada has been crafting the superb aesthetics of protest, beautifully illustrated in this challenge to anti-immigrant prejudice." —*Library Journal*

"*Floaters* proves [Espada] is the greatest living American poet. . . . Every poem in this book is a call to action, a commitment to change. . . . Espada reminds me to pay attention, to see, to listen, to act, to keep calling out injustice, to continue naming the dead, and to sing from right here, right now." —Dante Di Stefano, *Southern Humanities Review*

"All poetry carries the possibility for incantatory magic, but on Espada's tongue it is especially potent. . . . *Floaters* is itself a promise that poetry does indeed have the power to save us, a promise between the word and the world." —J. D. Schraffenberger, *North American Review*

"The visionary latest from Espada combines a sharp political awareness with a storyteller's knack for finding beauty and irony in the current moment. . . . Drawing on history, personal experience, and keen observation, this impressive collection is unique for the way it captures the world-weary voice of a poet and political activist who doesn't simply call for change, but offers a sense of the long, difficult struggle toward justice." —*Publishers Weekly*

"Although Espada knows how to bring light and heat to the current, heart-wrenching climate, he also evokes a speaker who, even in nostalgia or sadness, makes the reader laugh out aloud. . . . What unifies this collection of elegies, activism, and aubades may be summed up in one word: hope."

—Maria Nazos, *Massachusetts Review*

"A Latinx person who reads this will feel this book hitting home, and those who are not Latinx are invited to learn and understand."

—Natalie Ruiz-Pérez, *Vox*

"The book runs the gamut from scathing socio-political commentaries on the state of cultural affairs, particularly during the Trump era, to poignant homage to family, love, and poetic influence. These visceral poems, at turns both sardonic and breathtaking, reflect the author's commitment to immigrants' rights, social justice, and Puerto Rico. . . . It is a necessary, evocative read."

—Marian Perales, *Latino Book Review*

"Both elegiac and irrepressible, this is an essential read for anyone interested in poetry as a form of protest."

—*Chicago Review of Books*

"Espada brings injustice to the forefront . . . but it is his dignifying of immigrants and the disenfranchised that erupts throughout the collection with rhythmic cadences and vivid imagery. . . . These poems, however, are not merely snapshots of today's political moment. They timelessly capture both sorrow and beauty."

—Sheryl Luna, *Plough Quarterly*

"The poems are all limpidly beautiful, even when they speak of ugly behaviour and circumstances. . . . [T]he book is a history lesson as well as an aesthetic delight."

—Alan Dent, *Northern Review of Books* (UK)

"Vintage Espada—essential, topical, political, irrepressible; in his poems, mercy acquires muscle and close attention confers value—reminding us that protest and praise rise from the same source. Such eloquence in comradeship, elegy and homage to those who lit the path, and, oh, a fresh bounty of love poems, written 'not in lust but in astonishment.' "   —Eleanor Wilner

"Along with his trademark blend of gravitas, humor, and raucous imagination, we get an Espada more vulnerable, a voice more intimate, than any we've heard from him before. Martín Espada has long established himself as one of our most prolific and important poets, his body of work a canon unto itself. *Floaters* is another cannon in that canon."   —John Murillo

"In his dynamic new book, Martín Espada is a fierce activist in verse, decrying, with accuracy and urgency, the depravity of inhumane detention and acute bigotry. One of America's most indelible voices, as always, Espada's poetry is lionhearted."   —Cyrus Cassells

"If Martín Espada's name weren't on the book, I would still recognize the poems as his, the stories that so exactly capture the shaping moments of his life and the lives of others, resonant, particular and yet universal, rendered into a lovely, unique lyricism—with a hard-won maturity. The title poem does what Espada is called to do, naming the dead, saving the memory of their lives. This book disturbs in the best way, and still it sings."   —Wayne Karlin

Floaters

Floaters

POEMS

Martín Espada

W. W. NORTON & COMPANY
Independent Publishers Since 1923

For information about permission to reproduce selections from this book, write to
Permissions, W. W. Norton & Company, Inc., 500 Fifth Avenue, New York, NY 10110

For information about special discounts for bulk purchases, please contact
W. W. Norton Special Sales at specialsales@wwnorton.com or 800-233-4830

Manufacturing by Versa Press
Production manager: Julia Druskin

Library of Congress Cataloging-in-Publication Data

Names: Espada, Martín, date– author.
Title: Floaters : poems / Martín Espada.
Description: First edition. | New York, NY : W. W. Norton & Company, [2021]
Identifiers: LCCN 2020027736 | ISBN 9780393541038 (hardcover) |
ISBN 9780393541045 (epub)
Subjects: LCGFT: Poetry.
Classification: LCC PS3555.S53 F58 2021 | DDC 811/.54—dc23
LC record available at https://lccn.loc.gov/2020027736

ISBN 978-1-324-02181-0 pbk.

W. W. Norton & Company, Inc., 500 Fifth Avenue, New York, N.Y. 10110
www.wwnorton.com

W. W. Norton & Company Ltd., 15 Carlisle Street, London W1D 3BS

3 4 5 6 7 8 9 0

Dedicated to Lauren Marie Espada

Contents

I. Jumping Off the Mystic Tobin Bridge

II. Asking Questions of the Moon

III. Love Song of the Kraken

IV. Morir Soñando

Acknowledgments

These poems have appeared or will appear in the following publications, to whose editors grateful acknowledgment is made:

The Best American Poetry 2019 (Scribner): "I Now Pronounce You Dead"

The Brooklyn Rail: "Morir Soñando"

The Eloquent Poem: 128 Contemporary Poems and Their Making (Persea): "Love Song of the Kraken"

Guernica: "The Bard Shakes the Snow From the Trees"; "I Would Steal a Car for You"; "The Cannon on the Hood of My Father's Car"

Labor: Studies in Working-Class History: "Remake of Me the Sickle for Thy Grain"

The Massachusetts Review: "I Now Pronounce You Dead"

The Night's Magician: Poems About the Moon (Negative Capability): "Asking Questions of the Moon"

Nimrod: "Be There When They Swarm Me"; "That We Will Sing"

North American Review: "Jumping Off the Mystic Tobin Bridge"; "Aubade With Concussion"; "Love is a Luminous Insect at the Window"

Morning Star (UK): "Not for Him the Fiery Lake of the False Prophet"

80grados (Puerto Rico): "Morir Soñando"; "The Five Horses of Doctor Ramón Emeterio Betances"

Pangyrus: "The Stoplight at the Corner Where Somebody Had to Die"

Paterson Literary Review: "I Now Pronounce You Dead"; "Jumping Off the Mystic Tobin Bridge"; "Flan"; "Floaters"; "Aubade With Concussion"; "Insulting the Prince"

Poem-a-Day: "The Five Horses of Doctor Ramón Emeterio Betances"

Poems from Pandemia (Southword, Ireland): "The Five Horses of Doctor Ramón Emeterio Betances"

Poetry: "Letter to My Father"; "Jumping Off the Mystic Tobin Bridge"; "Flan"; "Aubade With Concussion"; "Not for Him the Fiery Lake of the False Prophet"; "The Assassination of the Landlord's Purple Vintage 1976 Monte Carlo"; "Standing on the Bridge at Dolceacqua"; "Floaters"

Portside: "Morir Soñando"

Prairie Schooner: "Mazen Sleeps With His Foot on the Floor"; "Death Rides the Elevator in Brooklyn"; "Boxer Wears America 1ˢᵗ Shorts in Bout With Mexican, Finishes Second"; "Love Song of the Galápagos Tortoise"

The Progressive: "Ode to the Soccer Ball Sailing Over a Barbed Wire Fence"

Rattle (Poets Respond): "Morir Soñando"

Smartish Pace: "Why I Wait for the Soggy Tarantula of Spinach"

El Sol Latino: "Morir Soñando"; "The Five Horses of Doctor Ramón Emeterio Betances"

What Saves Us: Poems of Empathy and Outrage in the Age of Trump (Curbstone/Northwestern): "Letter to My Father"

Many thanks to those who supported this work, especially Julia Alvarez, Brandon Amico, Doug Anderson, Dennis Bernstein, Jill Bialosky, Richard Blanco, Cyrus Cassells, Denise Chávez, Gisela Conn, Fred Courtright, Suzanne Daly, Jim Daniels, Kwame Dawes, Chard deNiord, Dante Di Stefano, Lauren Marie Espada, Marilyn Espada, Martin Farawell, Bill Fisher, Danielle Legros Georges, Maria Mazziotti Gillan, Donald Hall, Everett Hoagland,

Lawrence Joseph, Frances Lucerna, Eileen Mariani, Paul Mariani, Richard Michelson, John Murillo, Mazen Naous, Maria Nazos, Marilyn Nelson, Alicia Ostriker, Camilo Pérez-Bustillo, Allen Ruff, César Salgado, Luke Salisbury, Óscar Sarmiento, Jeremy Schraffenberger, Gary Soto, Maritza Stanchich, Leah Umansky, Rich Villar and Eleanor Wilner.

Many thanks also to the Poetry Foundation for the 2018 Ruth Lilly Poetry Prize, to the Academy of American Poets for a 2018 fellowship, to John Brown Lives for the 2018 Spirit of John Brown Freedom Award, and to the Bread and Roses Heritage Committee for the 2020 Bread and Roses Hall of Fame Award.

Naomi Ayala, excerpt from "Poverty" from *Wild Animals on the Moon & Other Poems* (Curbstone Press, 1997) is reprinted with the permission of the author.

Excerpt from "Afterwards" translated by Cola Franzen from *Poem of the Deep Song* in *Collected Poems* by Federico García Lorca, edited and translated by Christopher Maurer, copyright © 1991 by Christopher Maurer, is reprinted by permission of Farrar, Straus and Giroux.

Paul Mariani, excerpts from "A&P Nightshift: January 1959" from *Epitaphs for the Journey: New, Selected, and Revised Poems* (Cascade Books, 2012), *The Broken Tower: A Life of Hart Crane* (W. W. Norton, 1999), and "Hornet's Nest" from *Ordinary Time* (Slant / Wipf and Stock, 2020) are reprinted with the permission of the author.

I.

Jumping Off the Mystic Tobin Bridge

Jumping Off the Mystic Tobin Bridge

I close my eyes and see him windmilling his arms as he plummets from
the Mystic Tobin Bridge, to prove me wrong, to show me he was good,
to atone for sins like seeds in the lopsided apple of his heart, but mostly
to escape from me in the back of his cab, a Puerto Rican lawyer in a suit and tie.

I hated the 111 bus, sweltering in my suit and tie with the crowd in the aisle,
waiting to hit a bump on the Mystic Tobin Bridge so my head would finally
burst through the ceiling like a giraffe on a circus train. I hated the 111 bus
after eviction day in Chelsea District Court, translating the landlords and judges
into Spanish so the tenants knew they had to stuff their clothing into garbage
bags and steal away again, away from the 40-watt squint that followed them
everywhere, that followed me because I stood beside them in court. I would
daydream in the humidity of the bus, a basketball hero, flipping the balled-up
pages of the law into the wastebasket at the office as the legal aid lawyers
chanted my name. I hated the 111 bus. I had to take a taxicab that day.

What the hell you doing here? said the driver of the cab to me in my suit
and tie. *You gotta be careful in this neighborhood. There's a lotta Josés
around here.* The driver's great-grandfather staggered off a boat so his
great-grandson could one day drive me across the Mystic Tobin Bridge,
but there was no room in the taxi for chalk and a blackboard. He could
hear the sawing of my breath as I leaned into his ear, past the bulletproof
barricade somehow missing, and said: *I'm a José.* I could see the 40-watt
squint in his rearview mirror. *I'm Puerto Rican*, I said. It was exactly
5 PM, and we were stuck in traffic in a taxi on the Mystic Tobin Bridge.

The driver stammered his own *West Side Story* without the ballet,
how a Puerto Rican gang stole his cousin's wallet years ago. *You think
I'm gonna rob you?* I said, in my suit and tie, close enough now to tickle
his ear with the mouth of a revolver. I could hear the sawing of his breath.
He still wanted to know what I was doing there. *I'm a lawyer. I go to court
with all the Josés*, I said. Stalled traffic steamed around us, the breath
of cattle in the winter air. *Where you going for the holidays?* the driver said.
I thought about Christmas Eve in court, eviction orders flying from the judge's
bench when tenants without legal aid lawyers, or children old enough to translate
the English of the summons, did not answer to their names. Every year, the legal
aid lawyers told the joke about The Christmas Defense: *Your Honor, it's Christmas!*
I said to the driver: *I will be spending Christmas right here with my fellow Josés.*

The driver shouted: *What do you want me to do? Get out of this cab and jump off
the bridge?* We both knew what he meant. We both knew about Chuck Stuart,
the last man to jump off the Mystic Tobin Bridge. Everybody knew how Chuck
drove his wife to Mission Hill after birthing classes, the flash and pop in the dark
when he shot her in the head and himself in the belly. Everybody knew how
he conjured a Black carjacker on the crackling call to 911 the way the Mercury
Theater on the Air conjured Martians in New Jersey on the radio half a century
before. Everybody knew how a hundred cops pounded on door after door
in the projects of Mission Hill, locking a Black man in a cage for the world to see
like the last of his tribe on exhibit at the World's Fair. Everybody knew how
Chuck would have escaped, cashing the insurance check to drive away with
a new Nissan, but for his brother's confession, the accomplice throwing
the Gucci bag with makeup, the wedding rings and the gun off the Dizzy Bridge
in Revere. Everybody knew how Chuck parked his new car on the lower deck,
left a note and launched himself deep into the black water, how the cops
hauled his body from the river by lunchtime, when I walked into the office
to tell the secretary: *Chuck Stuart just jumped off the Mystic Tobin Bridge.*

I said nothing to the driver. I almost nodded *yes* in the rearview mirror. I confess, for a flash, I wanted him to jump. The driver, the cops, the landlords, the judges all wanted us to jump off the Mystic Tobin Bridge, all wanted us to sprout gills like movie monsters so we could paddle underwater back to the islands, down into the weeds and mud at the bottom, past the fish-plucked rib cages of the dead, the rusty revolvers of a thousand crimes unsolved, the wedding rings of marriages gone bad, till we washed up onshore in a tangle of seaweed, gasping for air.

Last night, still more landed here, clothing stuffed in garbage bags, to flee the god of hurricanes flinging their houses into the sky or the god of hunger slipping his knife between the ribs, not a dark tide like the tide of the Mystic River, but builders of bridges. You can walk across the bridges they build. Or you can jump.

Floaters

*Ok, I'm gonna go ahead and ask . . . have ya'll ever seen floaters this clean. I'm
not trying to be an a$$ but I HAVE NEVER SEEN FLOATERS LIKE THIS, could
this be another edited photo. We've all seen the dems and liberal parties do some
pretty sick things.* —ANONYMOUS POST, "I'M 10-15" BORDER PATROL FACEBOOK GROUP

Like a beer bottle thrown into the river by a boy too drunk to cry,
like the shard of a Styrofoam cup drained of coffee brown as the river,
like the plank of a fishing boat broken in half by the river, the dead float.
And the dead have a name: *floaters*, say the men of the Border Patrol,
keeping watch all night by the river, hearts pumping coffee as they say
the word *floaters*, soft as a bubble, hard as a shoe as it nudges the body,
to see if it breathes, to see if it moans, to see if it sits up and speaks.

And the dead have names, a feast day parade of names, names that
dress all in red, names that twirl skirts, names that blow whistles,
names that shake rattles, names that sing in praise of the saints:
Say *Óscar Alberto Martínez Ramírez.* Say *Angie Valeria Martínez Ávalos.*
See how they rise off the tongue, the calling of bird to bird somewhere
in the trees above our heads, trilling in the dark heart of the leaves.

Say what we know of them now they are dead: Óscar slapped dough
for pizza with oven-blistered fingers. Daughter Valeria sang, banging
a toy guitar. He slipped free of the apron he wore in the blast of the oven,
sold the motorcycle he would kick till it sputtered to life, counted off
pesos for the journey across the river, and the last of his twenty-five
years, and the last of her twenty-three months. There is another name
that beats its wings in the heart of the trees: Say *Tania Vanessa Ávalos*,
Óscar's wife and Valeria's mother, the witness stumbling along the river.

Now their names rise off her tongue: Say *Óscar y Valeria*. He swam
from Matamoros across to Brownsville, the girl slung around his neck,
stood her in the weeds on the Texas side of the river, swore to return
with her mother in hand, turning his back as fathers do who later say:
I turned around and she was gone. In the time it takes for a bird to hop
from branch to branch, Valeria jumped in the river after her father.
Maybe he called out her name as he swept her up from the river;
maybe the river drowned out his voice as the water swept them away.
Tania called out the names of the saints, but the saints drowsed
in the stupor of birds in the dark, their cages covered with blankets.
The men on patrol would never hear their pleas for asylum, watching
for *floaters*, hearts pumping coffee all night on the Texas side of the river.

No one, they say, had ever seen *floaters this clean*: Óscar's black shirt
yanked up to the armpits, Valeria's arm slung around her father's
neck even after the light left her eyes, both face down in the weeds,
back on the Mexican side of the river. *Another edited photo*: See how
her head disappears in his shirt, the waterlogged diaper bunched
in her pants, the blue of the blue cans. The radio warned us about
the *crisis actors* we see at one school shooting after another; the man
called *Óscar* will breathe, sit up, speak, tug the black shirt over
his head, shower off the mud and shake hands with the photographer.

Yet, the floaters did not float down the Río Grande like Olympians
showing off the backstroke, nor did their souls float up to Dallas,
land of rumored jobs and a president shot in the head as he waved
from his motorcade. No bubbles rose from their breath in the mud,
light as the iridescent circles of soap that would fascinate a two-year-old.

And the dead still have names, names that sing in praise of the saints,
names that flower in blossoms of white, a cortege of names dressed
all in black, trailing the coffins to the cemetery. Carve their names
in headlines and gravestones they would never know in the kitchens
of this cacophonous world. Enter their names in the book of names.
Say *Óscar Alberto Martínez Ramírez*; say *Angie Valeria Martínez Ávalos*.
Bury them in a corner of the cemetery named for the sainted archbishop
of the poor, shot in the heart saying mass, bullets bought by the taxes
I paid when I worked as a bouncer and fractured my hand forty years
ago, and bumper stickers read: *El Salvador is Spanish for Vietnam.*

When the last bubble of breath escapes the body, may the men
who speak of floaters, who have never seen floaters this clean,
float through the clouds to the heavens, where they paddle the air
as they wait for the saint who flips through the keys on his ring
like a drowsy janitor, till he fingers the key that turns the lock and shuts
the gate on their babble-tongued faces, and they plunge back to earth,
a shower of hailstones pelting the river, the Mexican side of the river.

Ode to the Soccer Ball Sailing Over a
Barbed-Wire Fence

Tornillo . . . has become the symbol of what may be the largest U.S. mass detention of children not charged with crimes since the World War II internment of Japanese-Americans. —ROBERT MOORE, *TEXAS MONTHLY*

Praise *Tornillo*: word for *screw* in Spanish, word for *jailer* in English,
word for three thousand adolescent migrants incarcerated in camp.

Praise the three thousand soccer balls gift-wrapped at Christmas,
as if raindrops in the desert inflated and bounced through the door.

Praise the soccer games rotating with a whistle every twenty minutes,
so three thousand adolescent migrants could take turns kicking a ball.

Praise the boys and girls who walked a thousand miles, blood caked
in their toes, yelling in Spanish and a dozen Mayan tongues on the field.

Praise the first teenager, brain ablaze like chili pepper Christmas lights,
to kick a soccer ball high over the chain-link and barbed-wire fence.

Praise the first teenager to scrawl a name and number on the face
of the ball, then boot it all the way to the dirt road on the other side.

Praise the smirk of teenagers at the jailers scooping up fugitive
soccer balls, jabbering about the ingratitude of teenagers at Christmas.

Praise the soccer ball sailing over the barbed-wire fence, white
and black like the moon, yellow like the sun, blue like the world.

Praise the soccer ball flying to the moon, flying to the sun, flying to other worlds, flying to Antigua Guatemala, where Starbucks buys coffee beans.

Praise the soccer ball bounding off the lawn at the White House, thudding off the president's head as he waves to absolutely no one.

Praise the piñata of the president's head, jellybeans pouring from his ears, enough to feed three thousand adolescents incarcerated at Tornillo.

Praise *Tornillo*: word in Spanish for adolescent migrant internment camp, abandoned by jailers in the desert, liberated by a blizzard of soccer balls.

Not for Him the Fiery Lake of the False Prophet

*When Mexico sends its people, they're not sending their best. . . . They're bringing
drugs. They're bringing crime. They're rapists.*   —DONALD TRUMP, JUNE 16, 2015

They woke him up by pissing in his face. He opened his mouth
to scream in Spanish, so his mouth became a urinal at the ballpark.

Scott and Steve: the Leader brothers, celebrating a night at Fenway,
where the Sox beat the Indians and a rookie named Rodríguez spun
the seams on his changeup to hypnotize the Tribe. Later that night,
Steve urinated on the door of his cell, and Scott told the cops why
they did it: *Donald Trump was right. All these illegals need to be deported.*

He was a Mexican in a sleeping bag outside JFK station on a night
in August, so they called him a *wetback* and emptied their bladders
in his hair. In court, the lawyers spoke his name: *Guillermo Rodríguez,*
immigrant with papers, crop-picker in the fields, trader of bottles
and cans collected in his cart. Two strangers squashed the cartilage
in his nose like a can drained of beer. In dreams, he would remember
the shoes digging into his rib cage, the pole raked repeatedly across
his cheekbones and upraised knuckles, the high-five over his body.

Donald Trump was right, said Scott. And Trump said: *The people
that are following me are very passionate.* His hands fluttered
as he spoke, a demagogue's hands, no blood under the fingernails,
no whiff of urine to scrub away. He would orchestrate the chant
of *Build that Wall* at rally after rally, bellowing till the blood rushed
to his face, red as a demagogue in the grip of masturbatory dreams:
a tribute to the new conquistador, the Wall raised up by Mexican hands,

Mexican hair and fingernails bristling in the brick, Mexican blood
swirling in the cement like raspberry syrup on a vanilla sundae.
On the Cinco de Mayo, he leered over a taco bowl at Trump Tower.

Not for him the fiery lake of the false prophet, reddening
his ruddy face. Not for him the devils of Puritan imagination,
shrieking in a foreign tongue and climbing in the window
like the immigrant demons he conjures for the crowd.
Not even for him ten thousand years of the Leader brothers,
streaming a fountain of piss in his face as he sputters forever.

For him, Hell is a country where the man in a hard hat
paving the road to JFK station sees Guillermo and dials 911;
Hell is a country where EMTs kneel to wrap a blanket around
the shivering shoulders of Guillermo and wipe his face clean;
Hell is a country where the nurse at the emergency room
hangs a morphine drip for Guillermo, so he can go back to sleep.
Two thousand miles away, someone leaves a trail of water bottles
in the desert for the border crossing of the next Guillermo.

We smuggle ourselves across the border of a demagogue's dreams:
Confederate generals on horseback tumble one by one into
the fiery lake of false prophets; into the fiery lake crumbles
the demolished Wall. Thousands stand, sledgehammers in hand,
to await the bullhorns and handcuffs, await the trembling revolvers.
In the full moon of the flashlight, every face interrogates the interrogator.
In the full moon of the flashlight, every face is the face of Guillermo.

Boxer Wears America 1st Shorts in Bout With Mexican, Finishes Second

—*HEADLINE IN THE* WASHINGTON POST, *APRIL 13, 2018*

In the blue corner, weighing 130 pounds, Lightning Rod Salka sheds his robe
to unveil *America* 1st emblazoned across the waistband, a wall of bricks
in the red, white and blue of the American flag stamped on his shorts.
He pivots and salutes the crowd. In the red corner, weighing 130 pounds,
El Bandido Vargas wears a black cowboy hat with a bandanna across his face.
His trainer slips them off. Eyebrow still healing from the last fight, El Bandido
studies Lightning Rod and his border wall trunks at the casino in Indio,
California. He cannot hear the ring announcer praise *Tecate, the beer of boxing,*
snarling: *Indio, are you ready?* The crowd buzzes at the clang of the bell.

Lightning Rod waves his hands in circles like a magician at a birthday party.
El Bandido hooks the belly. Lightning Rod jabs twice at the scarred eyebrow.
El Bandido hooks the belly. Lightning Rod paws and swats at the darkness.
El Bandido hooks the belly. Lightning Rod skips away, back against the ropes.
El Bandido hooks the belly. Lightning Rod is quiet in the corner between rounds.
El Bandido hooks the belly. Lightning Rod moans about low blows to the referee.

El Bandido hooks the belly, hooks the head, then snaps the uppercut to jolt
Lightning Rod back to a day when he was ten years old, watching a parakeet
in a pet shop tap a bell with his beak over and over again, and he spins around
in the corner, kneeling on the canvas, gloves on the ropes as if in prayer, as if
he forgets the wisecrack about boxers and God: *that only helps if you can fight.*

Lightning Rod quits in his corner, the welts stinging his body like red jellyfish, as the crowd hollers and jeers at the casino in Indio, California. Later, he says: *I'm not bigoted or racist.* I hear in my head a jingle on television back when I was ten years old, sung by a cartoon mustachioed Mexican in a sombrero to the tune of *Cielito Lindo: Ay, ay, ay ay, / I am the Frito Bandito. / I like Fritos Corn Chips, / I love them, I do. / I want Fritos Corn Chips, / I take them from you.*

Mazen Sleeps With His Foot on the Floor

for Mazen Naous

Mazen sleeps with his foot on the floor, trailing off the bed.
He does not dream of dancing in Beirut. He does not hear
his mother's oud, hanging on the wall, belly round like a pear
or fig or tear drop, strings cascading the ancient music.

Whenever the rockets and the bombs shook the house,
Mazen and his brother would jump from bed and sprint
to the basement. The first step could keep the boys one step
ahead of the ceilings and walls collapsing in dusty clouds
behind them. Mazen would sleep with his foot on the floor.
So he slept for fifteen years in the roaring music of Beirut.

I remember the air raid drills of my boyhood. The bald Russians
would bomb us. The bearded Cubans would bomb us. We stood
in the hallways at school, two lines facing the walls, because the bombs
would fall between us, in the middle of the hallway. The teachers told
us to be silent, and we were silent, except for the boy who chattered
at me until the music teacher who loved operettas and forced us
to listen smacked the boy into the wall. He was the only casualty.

The civil war in Lebanon is gone, and Mazen gone from Lebanon,
another teacher walking his dog on campus, navigating between
the chain-link fences with their cranes and boarded buildings,
signs everywhere in red warning *Danger.* At the airport in Boston,
Mazen's skin will glow as if saying *Danger,* and the wands will pass
over his body, scrutinized by agents who would rather scan his mind
for the clouds of bombs and rockets he conspires to drop on them.

Mazen still sleeps with his foot on the floor. He knows what we only
think we know, the civil war gone but not gone, how the first step
can save us when the walls dissolve like baking powder, even as we
block out the rumbling, staring hypnotized by the icy pond of the screen.

I Now Pronounce You Dead

for Sacco and Vanzetti, executed August 23, 1927

On the night of his execution, Bartolomeo Vanzetti, immigrant
from Italia, fishmonger, anarchist, shook the hand of Warden Hendry
and thanked him for everything. *I wish to forgive some people for what
they are now doing to me*, said Vanzetti, blindfolded, strapped down
to the chair that would shoot two thousand volts through his body.

The warden's eyes were wet. The warden's mouth was dry. The warden
heard his own voice croak: *Under the law I now pronounce you dead.*
No one could hear him. With the same hand that shook the hand
of Bartolomeo Vanzetti, Warden Hendry of Charlestown Prison
waved at the executioner, who gripped the switch to yank it down.

The walls of Charlestown Prison are gone, to ruin, to dust, to mist.
Where the prison stood there is a school; in the hallways, tongues
speak the Spanish of the Dominican, the Portuguese of Cabo Verde,
the Creole of Haiti. No one can hear the last words of Vanzetti,
or the howl of thousands on Boston Common when they knew.

After midnight, at the hour of the execution, Warden Hendry
sits in the cafeteria, his hand shaking as if shocked, rice flying off
his fork, so he cannot eat no matter how the hunger feeds on him,
muttering the words that only he can hear: *I now pronounce you dead.*

II.

Asking Questions of the Moon

The Story of How We Came to América

I remember the tale of my grandfather the gambler, tipped off
that the cops would raid his speakeasy, selling the club to another
gambler, fleeing Puerto Rico before somebody could press a gun
to his skull and scatter his brains through his white straw hat.

That is the story of how the Espada family came to América.
My father once said: *That never happened, and besides, you*
should wait till people are dead to tell stories like that.
Now people are dead, and I am telling stories like that.

Why I Wait for the Soggy Tarantula of Spinach

My mother and father met at Vera Scarves, the Brooklyn factory
in 1951. My mother was a receptionist, my father a shipping clerk.
She was twenty and would blush at pictures of Gregory Peck in movie
magazines; he was twenty-one and six foot four, one inch taller than
Gregory Peck. He asked her on a date to see *Captain Horatio Hornblower*,
starring Gregory Peck. They were standing at the corner of 7th Avenue
and 42nd Street in Times Square, waiting, hand in hand, for the red light
to glow green, when a soggy ball of spinach fell from the sky, landing
on my mother's head. I would say only God knows why, but He doesn't.
Maybe Popeye staged a mutiny, pouring his can of spinach overboard
instead of punching Bluto in the face again for the sake of Olive Oyl.
Maybe an eight-year-old boy who yearned to pitch for the Yankees
flipped a screwball of spinach out the window to shock his mother.

My mother's meticulously ironed curls wept green down her neck.
Her eyes wept too. My father was an airplane mechanic in the Air Force.
He knew what to do when something came plummeting from the sky.
Go down to the subway toilet, he said, *and rinse your hair in the sink.*
I'll wait for you up here. And so my mother did. She returned from
the subway toilet with hair wet and spiky, standing up like the crest
of a startled cockatoo. They went to see *Captain Horatio Hornblower*,
sat in the balcony and kissed throughout the movie, missing every line
of dialogue from Gregory Peck, wooing Virginia Mayo as Lady Barbara.

Once, I heard a poet deaf with age declaim a poem about seeing Halley's Comet as a boy in 1910. The ball of spinach was my mother's comet. Every day, my eyes scan the heavens, waiting for the soggy tarantula of spinach to plummet from the sky and splatter my thinning hair. This is my inheritance: not the spinach, but the certainty that spinach is hurtling at my head, or maybe a baby grand piano spinning from the clouds, and all I can do is wait. Only God knows why, but He doesn't.

The Stoplight at the Corner Where Somebody
   Had to Die

They won't put a stoplight on that corner till somebody dies, my father
would say. *Somebody has to die*. And my mother would always repeat:
Somebody has to die. One morning, I saw a boy from school facedown
in the street, there on the corner where somebody had to die. I saw
the blood streaming from his head, turning the black asphalt blacker.
He heard the bells from the ice cream truck and ran across the street,
somebody in the crowd said. *The guy in the car never saw him.*
And somebody in the crowd said: *Yeah. The guy never saw him.*

Later, I saw the boy in my gym class, standing in the corner of the gym.
Maybe he was a ghost, haunting the gym as I would sometimes haunt
the gym, standing in the corner, or maybe he wasn't dead at all. They
never put the stoplight there, at the corner where somebody had to die,
where the guy in the car never saw him, where the boy heard the bells.

Death Rides the Elevator in Brooklyn

On a winter morning in 1968, my father left to walk the picket line.
He rode the elevator in his black coat, hood over his head in the hour
before daybreak. On the third floor, the doors opened. A white man
waiting for the elevator stood there, peered at my father in his black
coat and hood, in his brown skin, then screamed and fled. The doors closed.

My father laughed on the picket line that morning. He laughed for years.
The guy thought I was Death, he would say. Death rides an elevator
in Brooklyn, mugger Death, militant Death, Puerto Rican Death.

Listening to the story, as the screaming man screamed louder with every
telling, I never thought one day my father would be the man standing
there, waiting for the elevator doors to open. He did not stare or scream
or run. He stepped into the elevator, and the doors closed behind him.

The Cannon on the Hood of My Father's Car

The football coach taught Driver's Ed. He would hear a siren pass and say:
There goes another one. He meant me. I mowed down the rubber cones
as if they marched at me, an orange army invading from an orange planet.
My head snapped with every curb I hit, a speed bag for the fist I never saw.

I failed Driver's Ed, *F* like father, *F* like Frank, my father's name. My father
now would have to teach me how to drive. He said: *I'd like to mount a cannon
on the hood of my car, swivel it around, and blast all the bad drivers off the road.*
He meant me. So I learned to drive, one eye on the quaking of his chin, the cords
in his neck, waiting for him to shred my learner's permit so it fluttered in my face.

A taxi dropped him off one morning. *You have to drive me back to the city,*
he said. *I lost my car.* At the age of five or so, I lost my turtle under the bed.
My father found the creature, crawling on his fingertips, still trying to escape.
JFK was president in 1962, but my father was the finder of lost turtles.

I tucked my learner's permit in my shirt pocket and drove him to the city.
I read the stubble on his chin. My father, who silenced the room whenever he
spoke, said nothing, years before the AA meeting where he stood up and said:
Hello, my name is Frank. We drove around the same block three times before
I said: *There it is.* Someone tore the cannon off the hood. That's why we missed it.

Asking Questions of the Moon

Some blind girls
ask questions of the moon
and spirals of weeping
rise through the air.
    —FEDERICO GARCÍA LORCA

As a boy, I stood guard in right field, lazily punching my glove,
keeping watch over the ballgame and the moon as it rose
from the infield, asking questions of the moon about the girl
with long blonde hair in the back of my classroom, who sat with me
when no one else would, who talked to me when no one else would,
who laughed at my jokes when no one else would, until the day
her friend sat beside us and whispered to her behind that long hair,
and the girl asked me, as softly as she could: *Are you a spic?*
And I, with a hive of words in my head, could only think to say:
Yes, I am. She never spoke to me again, and as I thought of her
in the outfield, the moon fell from the sky, tore through the webbing
of my glove, and smacked me in the eye. Blinded, I wept, kicked
the moon at my feet, and loudly blamed the webbing of my glove.

Standing on the Bridge at Dolceacqua

My only love sprung from my only hate!
—ROMEO AND JULIET, ACT 1, SCENE 5

At forty, I studied the mirror. I poked my mouth to free a trapped grain
of hamburger, and a tooth broke off between my fingers. I felt nothing.
The dentist said: *The tooth is dead. The root is dead. The X-rays show signs
of trauma to the lower jaw. What happened here?* I said: *Donald DeBlasio.*

Donald DeBlasio punched me in the mouth. I was fifteen. My lip split,
my skull clanged, and my body smacked the floor like a mannequin
in a store looted by rioters. He stood over me and grinned
as he would grin at me for the rest of my life. Whenever I saw
him, in the hallway at school or on the street, he would pump
his right fist in my face, slowly curling an invisible barbell.

He was a centurion guarding the last outpost of the empire,
another Sicilian or Calabrese fleeing Brooklyn for Valley Stream,
Long Island, escaping the barbarians who sacked Rome, back
from the dead in 1972 to steal their cars, torch their houses,
piss in their swimming pools, stab the boys, and kiss the girls.
I was a barbarian drifting far from his tribe, a Puerto Rican
without a knife in hand or a leather jacket ablaze in gang colors.
Everybody understood, even the teacher who glanced away the day
I was late and sat on the floor, so the front row could take turns
jabbing a shoe in my spine. I refused to worship their gods, Jesus
on the crucifix or the Yankees in the sacred arena of the Stadium,
or the football deity who could bench press 300 pounds and slammed
me into a locker whenever he saw me. He never said a word to me.
I never said a word to him. I learned to swallow blood and words.

For years, I would mimic their rooster strut, the sneering lip stuck out,
the bellowing battle cry of *bafangool.* I rooted against Rocky in all
the *Rocky* movies, cheering his choreographed pratfalls to the canvas.
When they rushed out the door of the pizza joint to gawk at the booming
car wreck on the corner, leaving my eggplant parm sub to burn black
in the oven, I called them *goombahs* and swore never to return.

I am sixty. The words flow over the wrinkled stone of my brain:
Dolceacqua, sweet water, fresh water, River Nervia in the province
of Imperia, region of Liguria. I stand on the bridge at Dolceacqua,
the same stone arch painted by Monet more than a century ago.
She contemplates the water gushing below the bridge, and I watch
at her shoulder to see the river as she sees the river, poet, teacher,
amati, like *amada* in Spanish, the word for beloved. Her mother's name
is Giovio, Calabrese from New Jersey, her grandfather a stone mason
before the beam rammed his head and the stroke crippled his right hand,
her great-grandmother a girl sewing buttons onto blouses who escaped
the Triangle Shirtwaist Factory fire, as others leapt, hand in hand, eyes shut,
from the ninth floor. I can no longer remember the curses in the poetry
of Shakespeare and Donald DeBlasio. She takes my hand, and leads me
across the bridge to the ruins of the castle on the other side of the river,
through the labyrinth of stone, up to the jagged battlements, where we
listen to the silence of the builders, and the birds, and the silence again.

III.

Love Song of the Kraken

Aubade With Concussion

Poverty is black ice.
　　　—NAOMI AYALA

You leave me sleeping in the dark. You kiss me and I stir,
fingers in your hair, eyes open, unseeing. You leave me asleep
every morning, commuting to the school in the city at sunrise.

The landlord's driveway, a muddy creek, ices over hard after
the freezing rain clatters all night. Your feet fly up, your head
slamming the ground, an eclipse of the sun flooding your eyes.
You sleep under the car. No one knows how long you sleep.

You awake with a hundred ice picks stabbing your eardrums.
You awake, coat and hair soaked, and somehow drive to school.
You remember to turn left at the Smith & Wesson factory.
The other teachers lead you by the elbow to Mercy Hospital,
where you pause when the nurse asks your name, where you claim
your pain level is a four, and they slide you into the white coffin
of an MRI machine. You hold your breath. They film your brain.

Concussion: the word we use for the boxer plunging face-first
to the canvas after the uppercut blindsided him, not the teacher
commuting to school at sunrise in a Subaru Crosstrek. Yet, you would
drive, ears hammering as they hammer in the purgatory of the MRI.

A week before, Isabela came to you in the classroom and said:
Miss, I cannot sleep. Three days, I cannot sleep. Her boyfriend called
at 2 AM, and she did not pick up. At 3 AM, a single shot to the head

put him to sleep, and he will sleep forever, his body hidden beneath
a car in a parking lot on Maple Street, the cops, the television cameras,
the neighbors all gathering at the yellow-tape carnival of his corpse.

You said to Isabela: *Take this journal. Write it down. You don't have
to show me. You don't have to show anyone.* On the cover of the journal
you bought at the drugstore was the word: *Dream.* Isabela sat there
in your classroom, at your desk, pencil waving in furious circles.
By lunchtime, as her friends slapped each other, Isabela slept,
head on the desk, face pressed against the pages of the journal.

This is why I watch you sleep at 3 AM, when the sleeping pills fail
to quell the strike meeting in my brain. This is why I say to you,
when you kiss me in my sleep: *Don't go. Don't go. You have to go.*

I Would Steal a Car for You

Papo stole a car so he wouldn't be late for school, the first bell
and the last chapter of the book you taught in English class.
He wanted to know how the story would end. His story ended
in handcuffs and jail, his gold star attendance record ruined.

I would steal a car for you, even though the keys no longer
dangle from the ignition as they did the year I was born.
I've never stolen a car, though I confess to vandalism,
ripping the hood ornament off a Mercedes to improvise
a belt buckle. My pants fell down anyway, leaving me
with skinned knees, a mouth spraying obscenities
and a story to tell. My pants still fall down today,
and you laugh till your face turns birthday-balloon pink,
so I do it again, a rodeo clown rehearsing the rescue
of the cowboy from the horns of a charging bull.

I may be sixty-two, but I wish I could steal a car for you.
You would spin the wheel and parallel park, graceful
as an ice skater gliding backwards in a figure eight.
I would have a story to tell, not a story where I play
all the parts with all the voices, only to learn that
you've heard the story a dozen times before. I would
steal a car to hear your stories, the tale of the boy
who stole a car so he would not be late for school.

I've heard the story many times before, but tell me
again about the first time we sat together and you knew
what all the crooners of all the ballads on all the car
radios in history could never find the words to sing:
I felt my blood flinch, you say. Tell me again how
you offered up a bag of raw almonds in your hand
and my fingers dipped into the bag. Tell me again
and again how we slow-danced in the parking lot
to the crooning of a Cuban ballad singer on the car radio.

That We Will Sing

I call you a saint, washing dishes at the soup kitchen, tutoring men
who cannot write their own names, teaching poetry to the addicts,
and I imagine Saint Sebastian, female and voluptuous this time,
no arrows this time, white robe slipping to her waist, writhing
in ecstasy at the touch of an invisible hand, green eyes cast
heavenward, though we know there is no God in Paterson.

Yet, in poetry class today, you gave the addicts a poem and they sang
the poem back to you, *Lift Every Voice and Sing*, and so they did,
even the man with one arm, and so their voices became human again,
not the baying of wolves to be shot on sight by police after sundown,
but church voices, school voices, voices before the needle flooded
their bodies and drowned all the songs, all the poems they knew.

I imagine Víctor Jara, rousing the crowd in Santiago de Chile to sing
the last verse of his peasant's prayer, *levántate y mírate las manos*,
rise up and look at your hands, how the crowd sang the song from
memory back to the singer, even the words he sang as if he could
foresee the coup, the officer's revolver in his ear, *ahora y en la hora
de nuestra muerte*, now and in the hour of our death, *amén*.

Afterwards, the addicts in a circle of folding chairs rose for you,
speaking of God in Paterson to their teacher the heretic, reaching
for your hands as if they could take the spirit in your skin back
to the shelter where they sleep tonight, touching you the way
I touch you sometimes, not in lust but in astonishment, telling
myself I did not imagine you, that you are here, that we will sing.

Love Song of the Kraken

Listen to the love song of the kraken.

Conquerors sailing the world mistake my body for an island.
They navigate into hurricanes and blame me when the ships vanish.
They hurl harpoons at my bulbous head as I slumber in the water.
They say I crave the crunch of oars and planks, peg legs and bone.
They say I am a monster. They say I am a squid. They say I am a myth.
When I fade into the sea after the shipwreck, no one calls my name.

Oh, listen to the love song of the kraken.

You snarl at the gawkers who stare at us strolling on the boardwalk.
You drowse in the embrace of my tentacles as I dangle off the couch.
You listen when I tell the epic kraken tales going back a thousand years.
You kiss the trail of the harpoons, and scrub the barnacles off my head.
You call my name when the sea takes me. You sunbathe on my island.

Yes, listen to the love song of the kraken.

Show me the armada of your enemies. Show me the admiral
in his admiral's pointy hat, leering at you from his spyglass.
Show me his babbling shipmates. Show me the sailor trembling
to light the fuse and fire the cannon. I will whip my tentacles
around their ships, hauling them to the murky bottom of the sea.

Let the insomniacs sedate themselves by listening to the whine
of whale song. Tonight, listen to the love song of the kraken.

Love Song of the Galápagos Tortoise

I am Lonesome George, the last Galápagos tortoise of Pinta Island.
I see Darwin's hairy face on T-shirts and hats, backpacks and mugs.
I see the statues. I can read the history books if someone turns the pages.

I remember Darwin. I was there the day he landed in the ship named
for a dog with floppy ears. He tried to lift me up and strained his groin.
He climbed on my saddleback shell and tried to ride me, giggling like
a boy on a birthday pony. He slipped off and rolled over in the surf,
spitting sand. He watched me plod around in search of cactus to crunch,
timing me with a pocket watch. He yelled in my ear to see if I was deaf,
and I hissed in his face. He invited my tortoise brothers and sisters
to board the *Beagle.* The crew hauled them up the gangplank as guests
of honor. Darwin noted in his journal: *Young tortoises make excellent soup.*
Like the pirates and the whalers, the naturalists licked their spoons,
soup in their beards, toasting the voyage with glasses of our urine.

I am Lonesome George. I crane my leathery neck and hiss at everyone.
I tuck my head inside my shell. You call and call my name till I peek out.
I am a creature of the tropics who curses the icebergs of December.
You dress me up in cardigan sweaters and wool scarves for winter.
I groan about my gut, intimidating the curious with a drumroll of flatulence.
You feed me the cactus of Pinta Island and pizza from the Jersey Shore.
I am afraid of the toaster and dream of Darwin's beard caught in its coils.
You are afraid of nothing, as you make waffles jump from the glowing machine.
I plod down the road as cars honk behind me, seafarers hungry for soup.

You let me steer the car, even though the world is blurry and you yell
in my ear when the other cars cruise like pirate ships through stop signs.

I will hiss at the next TV reporter who calls me Lonesome George. This world
teems with pirates, whalers and naturalists on parade, waving their spoons
in the air, craving the delicacy of buttery tortoise flesh, but now I crane
my neck to croak the love song of the Galápagos tortoise for you, and you
swear I am your Frank Sinatra, I am your Sam Cooke, I sing better than Darwin.

Love is a Luminous Insect at the Window

for Lauren Marie Espada
JUNE 13, 2019

The word *love*: there it is again, indestructible as an insect,
fly faster than the swatter, mosquito darting through the net.
How the word *love* chirps in every song, crickets keeping
a city boy up all night. I wish I could fry and eat them.
How the word *love* buzzes in sonnet after sonnet. I am
the beekeeper who wakes from a nightmare of beehives.
To quote Durán, the Panamanian brawler who waved a glove
and walked away in the middle of a fight: *No más. No more.*

Then I see you, watching the violinist, his eyes shut, the Russian
composer's concerto in his head, white horsehair fraying on the bow,
and your face is bright with tears, and there it is again, the word *love*,
not a fly or a mosquito, not a cricket or a bee, but the Luna moth
we saw one night, luminous green wings knocking at the screen
on the window as if to say *I have a week to live, let me in*, and I do.

Insulting the Prince

Monaco is a cake of many layers with a little prince on top.
—FRANCIS COMBES

We are wandering itinerant bards. Somehow, we wandered into Monaco,
and I gripped your hand, queasy in the back seat of the English teacher's
car as she spun the wheel, lost in her fantasies of winning the Grand Prix,
zipping past the tour buses, the yachts bristling in the harbor, the changing
of the guard at the palace, the crowds jostling for a glimpse of the monarch
in his white uniform. At lunch, you saw the official portrait of the prince
and his princess on the wall, his head bulging and hairless as an alien
from a science fiction movie, her grimace confirming the rumor that
she tried to flee the wedding, only to be captured by police at the airport.
It's like a bad prom picture, you said, and a *shush* arose from the teachers
at the table, the sound I never hear when I press a seashell to my ear.
Insulting the prince is against the law, they told us, and indeed
The Prince's persona is inviolable, says the constitution in Monaco.

At that moment, I remembered why I love your mouth, the kisses
but the curses too, the dialogue you memorized from the movies
at your father's video store in New Jersey, the lawbreaking words
that soared and tumbled like Olympic divers into the soup at lunch,
warned by the lifeguards of language, rattling the soup bowls again.

The Assassination of the Landlord's Purple Vintage
1976 Monte Carlo

The landlord says we have to go. On the night the thermostat read seventeen
below zero, and there was no heat on the first floor, the Massachusetts State
Sanitary Code appeared in the landlord's in-box like a spirit tapping bony
knuckles on his window, and a letter appeared in the landlord's in-box
like a spirit scratching the words *no rent* in the frost on his window,
and the landlord's mouth foamed as if he'd swallowed detergent,
and the foam froze on his beard, and the landlord's plumber laid
twenty-four feet of baseboard on the first floor, and now we have to go.

The landlord keeps his purple vintage 1976 Monte Carlo parked at the edge
of the driveway, purple inside and out, paint job and upholstery purple,
the color of emperors. The mad emperor Caligula assassinated his cousin,
jealous of his purple cloak, and the mad emperor's mouth foamed
as if he'd swallowed detergent, and the foam froze on his beard.

The neighbors report a moose sighting today. The moose charges from
the woods, mad as an emperor jealous of a purple cloak, sees the purple
vintage 1976 Monte Carlo as another moose, and rams Caligula's chariot
with his bristling antlers, kicking the car the way a teenager high on detergent
T-boned my leased Toyota Corolla two weeks ago, and so the moose claims
his territory, this land without a gas station or a movie theater or a pizza joint
or a doctor's office, and gallops back into the woods, snorting foam.

Now come the hunters tracking the moose, crossbows bristling since crossbow
season is upon us, their vision blurred by a night of Red Bull and detergent,
and see the purple vintage 1976 Monte Carlo as a moose, firing volley
after volley of arrows into the windshield, and the talisman of the air freshener
hanging from the rearview mirror does not keep the glass from exploding,
and the jumper cables coiled in the back seat do not rise magically like electric
eels, and the hunters explode in a cry of *huzzah*, waving their crossbows
as if their arrows thumped the hump of Richard the hunchback king.

The purple vintage 1976 Monte Carlo is a dead moose, tow truck dragging
away the carcass to a round of applause in my brain. The landlord will snort
and foam, demanding to know why there is nothing left but his mutilated
vanity plate stamped with the year *1976*, and I will speak to him in Brooklynese,
palms turned upward in the universal gesture of the uncooperative witness.
He will keep my security deposit, his territory without a gas station
or a movie theater or a pizza joint or a doctor's office. I say *huzzah*.

IV.

Morir Soñando

Remake of Me the Sickle for Thy Grain

for Arturo Giovannitti
Lawrence, Massachusetts, 1912

Remake of me the sickle for thy grain; remake of me the oven for thy bread.

The poet of the Bread and Roses strike, in his cravat and velvet vest,
messenger from the Industrial Workers of the World to the laborers
in the mills, spoke to them in Dante's tongue till they poured into
the streets as water pours from a shattered earthenware jug.

Remake of me the sickle for thy grain; remake of me the oven for thy bread.

Incitement to riot, accessory to murder, said the law after blood matted
the hair of a picketing girl shot by a cop. In the jailhouse where accused
witches once meditated on the same gallows, the poet carved in fountain pen
a poem in the voice of the iron bars that caged him at the feet of the judge:

Remake of me the sickle for thy grain; remake of me the oven for thy bread.

He rose from the cage in the courtroom, still wearing his cravat and vest,
speaking to the gallery in Shakespeare's tongue, till the reporters who
knew the creak of the gallows heard themselves sniffling in the distance,
and the sleeves of the jurors hid their eyes as the foreman said: *not guilty.*

Remake of me the sickle for thy grain; remake of me the oven for thy bread.

Whenever he would speak, the crowd became the chorus in his opera;
Helen Keller, socialist, typed in Braille the words to introduce his book;
he saw his own face smile stiffly back at him on one-cent postcards;
he loosened his cravat at meeting after meeting in the sweatshops.

Remake of me the sickle for thy grain; remake of me the oven for thy bread.

A century gone, the mills gone, the union gone, the books gone, the poet
faded as poets fade, like fountain pen, bedridden in a tenement room,
paralysis of the legs bewildering the doctor with his black bag, the bottle
of wine always by the bed, yet the iron in the bars of the cage still prays:

Remake of me the sickle for thy grain; remake of me the oven for thy bread.
Remake of me the sickle for thy grain; remake of me the oven for thy bread.

Be There When They Swarm Me

for Paul Mariani

You were once the boy of the big shoulders, hauling cartons
of Campbell's Soup at the A&P in 1959, yearning to brain
the boss with a wrench. You were the poet of the great handshake
and all the stories, squeezing my arm to tell me about Hart Crane,
who leapt from a ship to drown at sea: *Did he struggle
to regain the surface, suddenly sobered by what he'd done?*
I wandered lonely as a Puerto Rican in an English
Department, and you found me in the hallway,
calling me *brother* as my own brother never would,
calling me *poet* as if that word had never drowned at sea.
Once, I was a boy with big shoulders too, plotting
to shrink-wrap the foreman's head the night of the layoffs.
Not for you the poet learning to smoke like a poet,
bursting into tears at the sight of a mayonnaise jar
because he loves the letter *M*, locking himself
in the bathroom because his haiku is too short.

Now, you tell tales of the hospital bed, your *spine a wreck*,
your *wobbling brain.* Now, you write of scrubbing the deck
when hornets sting and zoom into your eyes, *as one winged fiend
multiplies by twenty*, and you win but know you cannot win,
and so you pray: *Be there when they swarm me.*

I wear a leg brace up to the knee. The surgeons
opened my belly like curious children inspecting

the pendulum of a grandfather clock. My insurance
will not pay for my hearing aids. At the airport,
they stop me because my beard is a suspect.

And yet, I will be there when they swarm you.
I will arm myself against the hornets with natural
insecticides, the eucalyptus oil, the citronella,
the spray of chrysanthemum flower tea, and then
the baseball bat, since I was born in Brooklyn,
where people used baseball bats to smash burglars,
cars, television screens, anything but baseballs.

We will win, though we know we cannot win.
You called me *brother* in the hallway as my brother
never would, spoke the word *poet* like a benediction,
and so we wait together for the next wave
of winged demons. *Be there when they swarm me.*

The Bard Shakes the Snow From the Trees

for Donald Hall (1928–2018)
Eagle Pond Farm, Wilmot, NH

Nearing ninety, the poet
in a Red Sox T-shirt
snarls the invocation
of the muse in ancient Greek,
digging the false teeth
from his jaw so the song
of the *Iliad* will escape
his beard and fly
up the chimney,
the roar of the bard
shaking the snow
from the trees
on Ragged Mountain.

Flan

for Jack Agüeros (1934–2014)

I was eight when the blackout struck and the lights died all across the city
like a massacre of fireflies. In the projects of Brooklyn, I steered myself
to 14F, fingers spread against the cool tiles of the hallway, past the concrete
and chicken-wire terrace where I once burnt ants with a magnifying glass.

Many years later, at the Chinese restaurant uptown, Jack said: *They got
any flan here?* He was my first poet. I had seen the fireflies in his sonnets
blink and float away: Fulano the philosopher in the unemployment line;
Blanco the painter, painting in the madhouse; Monterosa the dealer killed
by shotgun in a bar on Avenue A; his mother the seamstress and the quick
needle of her sewing machine; Jack the moving man, his hands sliced raw.
He stacked his apartment with dictionaries in three languages. I knew
the raconteur's grin with every tale: *Raúl Juliá is a friend of mine:
a Puerto Rican playing Macbeth. He took 14 curtain calls on opening night.*

Maybe he would tell me now that flan was not Puerto Rican, or Mexican,
or Spanish, but Chinese, invented by a trembling cook to satisfy the palate
of an emperor in the Ming Dynasty. *No flan, Jack*, I said. *This is a Chinese
restaurant.* Two minutes later, he said: *They got any flan?* I showed him
the dog-eared and fingerprinted menu. *No flan*, I said. When the waiter
unfurled his pad, Jack said to him: *You got flan?* He sang this song for an hour.
The egg roll was not flan. The fried rice was not flan. The fortune cookie
was not flan. *Can we get some flan?* he said. *Goddammit, Jack*, I said.

The poets crowded into the bar, striding to the mike. Jack stood with poem in hand, read the title, tilted his head and said it again, studied the page as if the words shriveled up like ants burnt under a magnifying glass, then sat down. I witnessed the massacre of fireflies. A few of us clapped, not knowing what to do with our hands, staring at the sonneteer who lost all his quatrains and couplets in the denim jacket he left on the subway, the words of Fulano still waiting on the unemployment line: *The faster you spin, the stiller you look. / There's something to learn in that, but what?*

After the diagnosis, I handed Jack a book of poems. He dangled the book upside down like a stiff mouse by the tail, something we would sniff behind the refrigerator. I wanted sonnets. Jack kept singing the chorus of a song: *Get me to the church. Get me to the church. Get me to the church on time.*

At the end, I leaned over Jack's bed to read his own poem in his ear, but some words come home after the blackout, fingers crawling on the wall. I know what I should have said at the Chinese restaurant: *Jack, let's get some flan.* We should have braved the subway at rush hour, straphangers rocking all the way to 14th Street and 8th Avenue, to La Taza de Oro, gone now like Jack, for rice and beans, squid in its own ink, café con leche y flan, Jack: a spoonful of flan for you after all the years of sonnets and bread for me, the steam rising when your hands cracked the crust at the table.

Morir Soñando

for Luis Garden Acosta (1945–2019)
Brooklyn, New York

I saw the empty cross atop the empty church on South 4th Street, as if Jesus
flapped his arms and flew away, spooked by one ambulance siren too many.
I saw the stained-glass windows I wanted to break with a brick, the mural
of Saint Mary and the Angels hovering innocent as spies over the congregation,
and wanted to know why you brought me here, the son of a man punched
in the face by a priest for questioning the Trinity, who punched him back.

This is El Puente, you said. *The Bridge.* I knew about the Williamsburg Bridge,
eight lanes of traffic and the subway stampeding in the open windows of the barrio
all summer. You spread your arms in that abandoned church and saw the spinning
of a carousel better than any wooden horses pumping up and down at Coney Island:
here the ESL classes for the neighbors cursed with swollen tongues in English;
there the clinics on contraception, the pestilence in the veins of the unsuspecting;
here the karate lessons, feet spearing the air to keep schoolyard demons away;
there the dancers in white, swirling their skirts to the drumming of bomba;
here the workshops on Puerto Rican history, La Masacre de Ponce where your
mother's beloved painted his last words on the street with a fingertip of blood.

I was a law student, first year, memorizing law school Latin, listening to classical
guitar on my boom box as I studied the rules of property: *It's mine. It's not yours.*
I saw only what could be proven by a preponderance of the evidence: the church
abandoned by the church, the cross atop the church abandoned by the Son of God.
My belly empty as Saint Mary of the Angels, I told you I was hungry, and we left.

I wanted Chinese food, but you told me about the Chinese takeout down the block
where you stood behind a man who shrieked about the price of wonton soup,
left and returned with a can of gasoline, splashed it on the floor and pulled a box
of kitchen matches from his pocket. *Will you wait till I pick up my egg roll and pork
fried rice?* you said, with a high school teacher's exasperated authority, so he did.

You could talk an arsonist into postponing his inferno till you left with lunch,
but you couldn't raise the dead in the ER at Greenpoint Hospital, even in your suit
and tie. You couldn't convince the girl called Sugar to rise from the gurney after
the gunshot drained the blood from her body. You couldn't persuade the doctor who
peeled his gloves and shook his head to bring her back to life, telling him *do it again,*
an arsonist in medical scrubs trying to strike a wet match. You couldn't jump-start
the calliope in her heart so the carousel of horses would rise and fall and rise again.
Whenever you saw the gutted church, you would see the sheets of the gurney
dipped in red, all the gurneys rolling into the ER with a sacrifice of adolescents.

We walked to the luncheonette on Havemeyer Street. A red awning announced
Morir Soñando. To Die Dreaming, you said, *from the DR, my father's island.*
The boy at the counter who spoke no English, brown as my father, called Martín
like me, grinned the way you grinned at El Puente, once Saint Mary of the Angels.
He squeezed the oranges into a drizzle of juice with evaporated milk, cane sugar
and ice, shook the elixir and poured it till the froth spilled over the lip of the glass.
Foam freckled my snout as I raised my hand for another. Intoxicated by morir
soñando number three and the prophet gently rocking at my table, I had a vision:

ESL classes healing the jaws wired shut by English, clinics full of adolescents
studying the secrets of the body unspeakable in the kitchen or the confessional,
karate students landing bare feet on the mat with a thump and grunt in unison,

bomba dancers twirling to a song in praise of Yoruba gods abolished by the priests, the words of Puerto Rican rebels painted on the walls by brushes dipped in every color, pressed in the pages of notebooks by a generation condemned to amnesia.

Morir soñando: Luis, I know you died dreaming of South 4th Street, the banners that said *no* to the toxic waste plant down the block or the Navy bombarding an island of fishermen for target practice thousands of miles away. Morir soñando: I know you died dreaming of vejigantes, carnival máscaras bristling with horns that dangled with the angels at El Puente. Morir soñando: I know you died dreaming of the next El Puente. Morir soñando: I know you died dreaming of the hammer's claw, the drill whining to the screw, the dust like snow in a globe, then the shy genius raising her hand in the back of the room. Morir soñando: I know you died dreaming of the poets who stank of weed in the parking lot, then stood before the mike you electrified for them and rubbed their eyes when the faces in their poems gathered there, waiting for the first word, so we could all die dreaming, morir soñando, intoxicated by the elixir of the tongue, oh rocking prophet at my table.

The Five Horses of Doctor Ramón Emeterio Betances

MAYAGÜEZ, PUERTO RICO, 1856

I. The First Horse

Cholera swarmed unseen through the water, lurking in wells and fountains,
squirming in garbage and excrement, infinitesimal worms drilling the intestines,
till all the water and salt would pour from the body, till the body became a worm,
shriveling and writhing, a slug in salt, till the skin burned blue as flame, the skin
of the peasant and the skin of the slave gone blue, the skin in the slave barracks blue,
the skin of ten thousand slaves blue. The Blue Death, face hidden in a bandanna,
dug graves with the gravediggers, who fell into holes they shoveled for the dead.
The doctors died too, seeing the signs in the mirror, the hand with the razor shaking.

II. The Second Horse

Doctor Betances stepped off the boat, back from Paris, the humidity of the plague
glistening in his beard. He saw the stepmother who fed him sink into a mound
of dirt, her body empty as the husk of a locust in drought. He toweled off his hands.
In the quarantine tents, there was laudanum by the bitter spoonful, the lemonade
and broth; in the dim of the kerosene lamps there was the compress cool against
the forehead, the elixir of the bark from the cinchona tree. For peasants and slaves
moaning to their gods, the doctor prescribed chilled champagne to soothe the belly.
For the commander of the Spanish garrison, there was silence bitter as the spoon.

III. The Third Horse

At every hacienda, at every plantation, as the bodies of slaves rolled one by one
into ditches all hipbones and ribs, drained of water and salt, stripped of names,
Doctor Betances commanded the torch for the barracks where the bodies would

tangle together, stacked up as if they never left the ship that sailed from Africa,
kept awake by the ravenous worms of the plague feasting upon them. Watching
the blue flames blacken the wood, the doctor and the slaves saw another plague
burning away, the plague of manacles scraping the skin from hands that cut
the cane, the plague of the collar with four spikes for the runaways brought back.

IV. The Fourth Horse
The pestilence of the masters, stirred by spoons into the coffee of the world,
spread first at the marketplace, at auction, the coins passing from hand to hand.
So Doctor Betances began, at church, with twenty-five pesos in pieces of eight,
pirate coins dropped into the hands of slaves to drop into the hands of masters,
buying their own infants at the baptismal font. The secret society of abolitionists
shoved rowboats full of runaways off the docks in the bluest hour of the blue night,
off to islands without masters. Even the doctor would strangle in the executioner's
garrote, spittle in his beard, if the soldiers on watch woke up from the opiate of empire.

V. The Fifth Horse
The governor circled his name in the name of empire, so Doctor Betances
sailed away to exile, the island drowning in his sight, but a vision stung
his eyes like salt in the wind: in the world after the plague, no more
plague of manacles; after the pestilence, no more pestilence of masters;
after the cemeteries of cholera, no more collar of spikes or executioners.
In his eye burned the blue of the rebel flag and the rising of his island.
The legend calls him the doctor who exhausted five horses, sleepless
as he chased invisible armies into the night. Listen for the horses.

Letter to My Father

October 2017

You once said: *My reward for this life will be a thousand pounds of dirt shoveled in my face.* You were wrong. You are seven pounds of ashes in a box, a Puerto Rican flag wrapped around you, next to a red brick from the house in Utuado where you were born, all crammed together on my bookshelf. You taught me there is no God, no life after this life, so I know you are not watching me type this letter over my shoulder.

When I was a boy, you were God. I watched from the seventh floor of the projects as you walked down into the street to stop a public execution. A big man caught a small man stealing his car, and everyone in Brooklyn heard the car alarm wail of the condemned: *He's killing me.* At a word from you, the executioner's hand slipped from the hair of the thief. *The kid was high*, was all you said when you came back to us.

When I was a boy, and you were God, we flew to Puerto Rico. You said: *My grandfather was the mayor of Utuado. His name was Buenaventura. That means good fortune.* I believed in your grandfather's name. I heard the tree frogs chanting to each other all night. I saw banana leaf and elephant palm sprouting from the mountain's belly. I gnawed the mango's pit, and the sweet yellow hair stuck between my teeth. I said to you: *You came from another planet. How did you do it?* You said: *Every morning, just before I woke up, I saw the mountains.*

Every morning, I see the mountains. In Utuado, three sisters, all in their seventies, all bedridden, all Pentecostales who only left the house for church, lay sleeping on mattresses spread across the floor

when the hurricane gutted the mountain the way a butcher slices open
a dangled pig, and a rolling wall of mud buried them, leaving the fourth
sister to stagger into the street, screaming like an unheeded prophet
about the end of the world. In Utuado, a man who cultivated a garden
of aguacate and carambola, feeding the avocado and star fruit to his
nieces from New York, saw the trees in his garden beheaded all at once
like the soldiers of a beaten army, and so hanged himself. In Utuado,
a welder and a handyman rigged a pulley with a shopping cart to ferry
rice and beans across the river where the bridge collapsed, witnessed
the cart swaying above so many hands, then raised a sign that told
the helicopters: *Campamento los Olvidados: Camp of the Forgotten.*

Los olvidados wait seven hours in line for a government meal of Skittles
and Vienna sausage, or a tarp to cover the bones of a house with no roof,
as the fungus grows on their skin from sleeping on mattresses drenched
with the spit of the hurricane. They drink the brown water, waiting
for microscopic monsters in their bellies to visit plagues upon them.
A nurse says: *These people are going to have an epidemic. These people
are going to die.* The president flips rolls of paper towels to a crowd
at a church in Guaynabo, Zeus lobbing thunderbolts on the locked ward
of his delusions. Down the block, cousin Ricardo, Bernice's boy, says
that somebody stole his can of diesel. I heard somebody ask you once
what Puerto Rico needed to be free. And you said: *Tres pulgadas
de sangre en la calle: Three inches of blood in the street.* Now, three
inches of mud flow through the streets of Utuado, and troops patrol
the town, as if guarding the vein of copper in the ground, as if a shovel
digging graves in the backyard might strike the ore below, as if la brigada
swinging machetes to clear the road might remember the last uprising.

I know you are not God. I have the proof: seven pounds of ashes in a box on my bookshelf. Gods do not die, and yet I want you to be God again. Stride from the crowd to seize the president's arm before another roll of paper towels sails away. Thunder Spanish obscenities in his face. Banish him to a roofless rainstorm in Utuado, so he unravels, one soaked sheet after another, till there is nothing left but his cardboard heart.

I promised myself I would stop talking to you, white box of grey grit. You were deaf even before you died. Hear my promise now: I will take you to the mountains, where houses lost like ships at sea rise blue and yellow from the mud. I will open my hands. I will scatter your ashes in Utuado.

Note on the Cover Photograph

My father, Frank Espada, was a documentary photographer and the creator of the Puerto Rican Diaspora Documentary Project, a photo documentary and oral history of the Puerto Rican migration. The project resulted in more than forty solo exhibitions and a book entitled *The Puerto Rican Diaspora: Themes in the Survival of a People* (2006). His work is included in the collections of the Smithsonian National Museum of American History, the Smithsonian American Art Museum, the National Portrait Gallery, and the Library of Congress.

One of my father's photographs appears on the cover of this book. This is *Angel Luis Jiménez, Evicted Mushroom Worker, Kennett Square, PA, 1981*. A migrant from Caguas, Puerto Rico, Jiménez had nine children; in the photograph, he is explaining his eviction. He said: "Aquí venimos a pasar hambre y amarguras" ("We come here to suffer hunger and bitterness"). The quotation would appear on the wall next to the photograph in my father's exhibitions.

The photograph reflects many subjects and themes of the poetry: migrants and migration, the dead and the hunger that drove them to swim across borders, the evicted tenants I represented as a lawyer, the young people playing soccer in an internment camp, my wife's high school students, the victims and survivors of hurricanes, and my father, himself a migrant to this country, who would one day speak for others like him through his art.

Notes on the Poems

Jumping Off the Mystic Tobin Bridge: From 1987 to 1993, I served as supervisor of Su Clínica Legal, a legal services program for low-income, Spanish-speaking tenants in Chelsea, outside Boston. Stanza five refers to Chuck Stuart, who shot and killed his pregnant wife, Carol DiMaiti Stuart, on October 23, 1989, blamed the killing on an invented African American carjacker, then committed suicide when his brother Matthew confessed his complicity and identified Chuck as the killer. This section of the poem relies in part on "Charles Stuart's Awful Legacy, In Black and White," by Adrian Walker, in the *Boston Globe*, October 24, 2014.

Floaters: Óscar Alberto Martínez Ramírez and Angie Valeria Martínez Ávalos, a migrant father and daughter from El Salvador, drowned crossing the Río Grande between Matamoros, México, and Brownsville, Texas, on June 23, 2019. Julia Le Duc, a journalist with the Mexican newspaper *La Jornada*, photographed their bodies the following day, reporting the eyewitness account of Tania Vanessa Ávalos, Óscar's wife and Valería's mother. The photograph went everywhere, appearing on the front page of the *New York Times*. An anonymous post on the page of the "I'm 10-15" Border Patrol Facebook group, representing nearly ten thousand current and former Border Patrol agents, alleged that the photograph had been doctored or staged. "Floaters" is the term often used by Border Patrol agents to describe those who have drowned attempting to cross. "The archbishop of the poor" refers to Óscar Romero, the archbishop of San Salvador, a champion of human rights assassinated by a right-wing gunman while saying mass on March 24, 1980. The poem relies in part on several background sources: "'They Wanted the American Dream': reporter reveals story behind tragic photo" by Julia Le Duc, in the *Guardian*, June 25, 2019; "Here's the Story Behind the Horrific Photo of the Man and Toddler Drowning at the Border" by Amanda Kaufman, in the *Boston Globe*, June 26, 2019; "Óscar y Valeria, despedidos entre oraciones y homenajes durante entierro" by Diana Escalante, in *El Salvador.com*, July 2, 2019; "Dan el ultimo adiós a Óscar y Angie Valeria en panteón de San Salvador" by Agent France-Presse, in *La Jornada*, July 2, 2019; and "Inside the Secret Border Patrol Facebook Group Where Agents Joke About Migrant Deaths and Post Sexist Memes" by A. C. Thompson, in *ProPublica*, July 1, 2019.

Ode to the Soccer Ball Sailing Over a Barbed Wire Fence: The epigraph comes from "Tent City Operator's Request for Policy Shift Could Reduce the Mass Detention of Migrant Children" by Robert Moore, in *Texas Monthly*, December 15, 2018. This poem relies in part on personal conversations and emails with Camilo Pérez-Bustillo, former advocacy director of the Hope Border Institute in El Paso, Texas, and an organizer of the successful campaign to shut down the camp, who interviewed incarcerated migrant children at the Tornillo camp.

Not for Him the Fiery Lake of the False Prophet: In the early hours of August 19, 2015, two South Boston brothers, Scott and Steve Leader, beat a homeless Mexican man, Guillermo Rodríguez, they found sleeping outside the JFK subway station on the Red Line. The brothers pleaded guilty and were sentenced to three and two and a half years in prison, respectively. "Rodríguez" in stanza one refers to Eduardo Rodríguez, Venezuelan-born pitcher for the Boston Red Sox. The quotes from Scott Leader and Donald Trump in stanzas two and four come from "South Boston Brothers Allegedly Beat Homeless Man" by Sara DiNatale and Maria Sacchetti, in the *Boston Globe*, August 19, 2015. The epigraph comes from "Here's Donald Trump's Presidential Announcement Speech" by *Time* staff in *Time* magazine, June 16, 2015.

Boxer Wears America 1ˢᵗ Shorts in Bout With Mexican, Finishes Second: The title comes from an article of the same name in the *Washington Post* by Matt Bonesteel, April 13, 2018. Born in Ciudad de México, Francisco "El Bandido" Vargas was World Boxing Council super featherweight champion (2015–17). The "Frito Bandito" was the cartoon mascot for Fritos Corn Chips from 1967 through 1971.

Mazen Sleeps With His Foot on the Floor: Mazen Naous is a professor of English at the University of Massachusetts Amherst and the author of *Poetics of Visibility in the Contemporary Arab American Novel* (Ohio State University Press, 2020). This poem is based on personal conversations about his experiences growing up in Beirut during the civil war in Lebanon (1975–90). An "oud," from the Arabic, is a stringed instrument similar to the lute used in the music of the Middle East and North Africa.

I Now Pronounce You Dead: In April 1920, a payroll robbery occurred at a shoe factory in South Braintree, Massachusetts, resulting in the murder of a paymaster and a payroll guard. Two Italian anarchists, Nicola Sacco, a shoemaker, and Bartolomeo Vanzetti, a fish peddler, were tried and convicted in an atmosphere of anti-immigrant bigotry and political hysteria. An international movement arose to free them; the judge, Webster Thayer, referred to the defendants as "anarchist bastards" and denied repeated motions for a new trial. The quotations from Vanzetti, Warden William Hendry and other details of the execution in the first two stanzas come from "Sacco and Vanzetti Put to Death Early This Morning" in the *New York Times*, August 23, 1927. The former site of Charlestown State Prison in Boston, where Sacco and Vanzetti were executed, is now the site of Bunker Hill Community College, a school with a large immigrant population.

Why I Wait for the Soggy Tarantula of Spinach: In the third stanza, the lines "I heard a poet deaf with age declaim a poem about seeing Halley's / Comet as a boy in 1910" refer to Stanley Kunitz reading his poem "Halley's Comet" from *The Collected Poems: Stanley Kunitz* (W. W. Norton, 2000).

Asking Questions of the Moon: The epigraph comes from "Después de pasar" ("Afterwards") in the *Poema del cante jondo* (*Poem of the Deep Song*) by Federico García Lorca, translated by Cola Franzen in the *Collected Poems* (Farrar, Straus and Giroux, 1991).

Standing on the Bridge at Dolceacqua: Dolceaqua is a winemaking village in northwestern Italy, on the border with France. Claude Monet painted *Dolceacqua, Bridge*, in 1884. On March 25, 1911, the Triangle Shirtwaist Factory fire in New York killed 146 garment workers, mostly women and girls. Many of them jumped to their deaths.

Aubade With Concussion: An "aubade," from the French, is a poem or song about lovers parting at dawn. The epigraph comes from the poem "Poverty" in *Wild Animals on the Moon* by Naomi Ayala (Curbstone Press, 1997).

I Would Steal a Car for You: "the crooning of a Cuban ballad singer on the car radio" refers to Ibrahim Ferrer of the Buena Vista Social Club, singing "Dos gardenias."

That We Will Sing: The poem refers to Eva's Village, an antipoverty organization with a residential substance abuse recovery program, serving mostly African American and Latinx clients in Paterson, New Jersey. "Lift Every Voice and Sing," a poem written by James Weldon Johnson and set to music by his brother John Rosamond Johnson in 1900, came to be known as the Black National Anthem. The third stanza quotes "Plegaria a un labrador," or "Prayer to a Peasant," by the legendary singer-songwriter and guitarist Víctor Jara of Chile. In the days following the military coup on September 11, 1973, Jara was tortured and shot dead at Estadio Chile in Santiago. Four years earlier, in July 1969, Jara received First Prize at the Festival de la Nueva Canción Chilena (Chilean New Song Festival) for "Plegaria a un labrador" at the same arena where he would ultimately be murdered. Estadio Chile has been renamed Estadio Víctor Jara.

Love Song of the Galápagos Tortoise: "Lonesome George" was considered the last surviving member of *Chelonoidis abingdonii*, a species of tortoise from Pinta Island in the Galápagos, when he died in 2012, aged more than one hundred years. Charles Darwin arrived on *The Beagle* in 1835. The first two stanzas rely in part on "Charles Darwin: Tortoise Hunter?" by Elizabeth Hennessy, published on the Yale University Press blog, November 18, 2019. Darwin's observation, "Young tortoises make excellent soup," comes from his journals: *The Works of Charles Darwin, Vol. 3, Journal of Researches, Part Two*, edited by Paul Barrett and R. B. Freeman (New York University Press, 1987).

Love is a Luminous Insect at the Window: "Durán, the Panamanian brawler" refers to Roberto Durán, the lightweight, welterweight, light middleweight and middleweight boxing champion, who allegedly uttered the words "No más" when he quit in his rematch with Sugar Ray Leonard. "The Russian composer's concerto" refers to the Violin Concerto in D Major, Opus 35 by Pyotr Ilyich Tchaikovsky. I read this sonnet at my wedding.

Insulting the Prince: The epigraph comes from a personal conversation with French poet and publisher Francis Combes. Stanza one refers to His Serene Highness Albert II, Sovereign Prince of Monaco, and Her Serene Highness Charlene, Princess of Monaco. Article 3 of the Constitution of the Principality provides that "The Prince's persona is inviolable."

Remake of Me the Sickle for Thy Grain: Arturo Giovannitti was an Italian poet, socialist, orator and labor organizer with the Industrial Workers of the World. Giovannitti was an organizer of the celebrated Bread and Roses strike in Lawrence, Massachusetts (January–March 1912). More than twenty thousand workers, mostly immigrants, walked out of the textile mills, and would ultimately prevail. When police shot and killed striker Anna LoPizzo at a parade on January 29, 1912, authorities charged Giovannitti and fellow strike leader Joseph Ettor as accessories to murder and put them on trial for their lives in a Salem, Massachusetts, courtroom, where they sat with codefendant Joseph Caruso in cages during the proceedings. The title and refrain quote two lines from "The Cage," written by Giovannitti at the time of his incarceration. Giovannitti and his codefendants were acquitted in November 1912. He published two books in 1914 with Hillacre Bookhouse: *The Cage* and a collection of poems called *Arrows in the Gale*, with an introduction by Helen Keller. The poem relies in part on *History of the Labor Movement in the United States, Vol. 4: The Industrial Workers of the World, 1905–1917* by Philip Foner (International Publishers, 1965) and *Rebel Voices: An IWW Anthology*, edited by Joyce Kornbluh (Charles H. Kerr Publishing Company, 1988).

Be There When They Swarm Me: Paul Mariani is a poet, essayist, biographer of poets, professor of English emeritus at Boston College and former professor of English at the University of Massachusetts Amherst. He is the author of twenty books, including eight collections of poetry and biographies of William Carlos Williams, Hart Crane, John Berryman, Wallace Stevens, Robert Lowell and Gerard Manley Hopkins. The first stanza of this poem refers to the subject of Mariani's poem "A&P Nightshift: January 1959" in his collection *Epitaphs for the Journey: New, Selected and Revised Poems* (Cascade Books, 2012). Stanza one also quotes *The Broken Tower: The Life of Hart Crane* (W. W. Norton, 1999). Stanza two quotes Mariani's poem "Hornet's Nest" from *Ordinary Time* (Slant/Wipf and Stock, 2020). The title and last line of my poem come from the Mariani poem.

The Bard Shakes the Snow From the Trees: Donald Hall (1928–2018) was a poet, editor, essayist and baseball writer. He published more than fifty books, including fifteen collections of poetry. He served as poet laureate of the United States (2006–7) and received numerous awards, ranging from the Ruth Lilly Poetry Prize to the National Medal of Arts. This poem is based on a visit with Hall at Eagle Pond Farm in Wilmot, New Hampshire, in February 2018, a few months before his death.

Flan: Jack Agüeros (1934–2014) was a Puerto Rican poet, fiction writer, essayist, playwright, translator, community organizer and director of El Museo del Barrio in East Harlem. He died of complications from Alzheimer's disease. I often referred to him as my "second father." He published three collections of poetry and one collection of short fiction, and translated *Song of the Simple Truth: The Complete Poems of Julia de Burgos* (Curbstone, 1997). Stanza two refers to the subjects of five Agüeros sonnets from *Correspondence Between the Stonehaulers* (Hanging Loose, 1991) and *Sonnets From the Puerto Rican* (Hanging Loose, 1996). Stanza four quotes the couplet from "Sonnet Substantially Like the Words of Fulano Rodríguez One Position Ahead of Me on the Unemployment Line." Raúl Juliá (1940–1994) was a film and theater actor from Puerto Rico who played Macbeth in the New York Shakespeare Festival's production at the Public Theater in 1990. La Taza de Oro ("The Cup of Gold") was a Puerto Rican restaurant in the Chelsea section of Manhattan from 1947 to 2015. "Café con leche" is coffee with steamed milk.

Morir Soñando: Luis Garden Acosta (1945–2019) was a major Puerto Rican/ Dominican activist, community organizer and cofounder of El Puente, a multiservice community center for adolescents and others in the Williamsburg section of Brooklyn. He was also an important mentor of mine. The poem is based on my visit with him to the abandoned church that would become El Puente in 1982, an encounter cited in "Luis Garden Acosta, Resuscitator of a Brooklyn Neighborhood, Dies at 73" by Sam Roberts, in the *New York Times*, January 11, 2019. "La Masacre de Ponce," or the Ponce Massacre, took place on March 21, 1937, in the city of Ponce, Puerto Rico, when police fired on a peaceful, proindependence Nationalist Party march, killing 21 people and wounding more than 200. "Morir soñando" means "to die dreaming." "Bomba" refers to a traditional form of Afro-Puerto Rican dance and percussion that originated on the sugar plantations of the island during the times of slavery. "Yoruba" refers to an ethnic group from West Africa. "Vejigantes" refers to costumed, masked figures at carnivals and festivals in Puerto Rico; the horned masks are considered emblematic of cultural identity.

The Five Horses of Doctor Ramón Emeterio Betances: Called the "Padre de la Patria" or the "Father of the Nation," Ramón Emeterio Betances (1827–1898) was a Puerto Rican revolutionary, abolitionist, essayist, novelist, diplomat and physician. Born in Cabo Rojo of partly African descent, he received his medical degree in Paris, returning in 1856 to a cholera epidemic in Puerto Rico that killed 25,000 to 30,000 people, including his stepmother, brother-in-law and approximately 10,000 under the yoke of slavery. He played a major role fighting the epidemic in the city of Mayagüez and elsewhere. Simultaneously, he emerged as an organizer of abolitionist "secret societies," for which he was forced into exile. Betances was the architect of an insurrection against the Spanish in 1868, called the "Grito de Lares," or "Battle Cry of Lares." (He even designed the rebel flag.) The insurrection failed, but slavery was abolished in 1873. The poem as a whole draws upon "Betances y la epidemia del cólera" by Mario Cancel-Sepúlveda in *Puerto Rico: su transformación en el tiempo* (Editorial Cordillera, 2008) and "En los tiempos del cólera" by Félix Ojeda Reyes from *Ramón Emeterio Betances: Obras completas (Vol. XIII), La Biografía I* (ZOOMIdeal, 2018). Stanza two relies in part on "Epidemia y sociedad: efectos del cólera morbo en Puerto Rico y en Costa Rica a mediados del siglo XIX" by Ramonita Vega Lugo in *IX Congreso Centroamericano de Historia* (Universidad de Costa Rica, 2008). Stanza four relies in part on "For the Freedom of Enslaved Infants in Puerto Rico, 1850s" by Virginia Sánchez Korrol in the *Huffington Post*, April 7, 2014.

Letter to My Father: My father, Frank Espada (1930–2014), was born in Utuado, Puerto Rico, a mountain town in the Cordillera Central. His grandfather, Buenaventura Roig, was the mayor, 1917–20, 1931–32 and 1939–40. After Hurricane María, Jon Lee Anderson wrote in *The New Yorker* (October 10, 2017) that Utuado "has become a byword for the island's devastation." The quotation in stanza five, "These people are going to have an epidemic. These people are going to die," comes from nurse Alicia Schwartz, cited in "These Volunteer Nurses in Puerto Rico Fear FEMA is Failing" by Jennifer Bendery, in the *Huffington Post*, October 16, 2017. (In August 2018, following a George Washington University study, governor Ricardo Rosselló revised the official death toll due to the hurricane from 64 to 2,975.) In stanza five, "las brigadas" refers to work brigades clearing away the wreckage, opening the roads to Utuado and more. "The last uprising" refers to "El Grito de Utuado" or "the Battle Cry of Utuado," a Nationalist rebellion for independence on October 30, 1950. The poem is based in part on personal conversations with my father and my cousin Gisela Conn. Stanzas four and five rely in part on several background sources, including "In One Puerto Rico Mountain Town, a Wall of Mud Came Crashing Down" by Molly Hennessey-Fiske, in the *Los Angeles Times*, September 24, 2017; "Stranded by Hurricane María, Puerto Ricans Get Creative to Survive" by Caitlin Dickerson, in the *New York Times*, October 16, 2017; "The 'Forgotten Ones': 37 Days After Hurricane María, Puerto Rico Neighborhood Still Stranded" by Kyra Gurney, in the *Miami Herald*, October 29, 2017; and an interview with Rosa Clemente by Amy Goodman, on *Democracy Now!*, October 18, 2017. I wrote the poem for a benefit, *#PoetsforPuertoRico: A Reading for Hurricane Relief*, at Poets House in New York on November 4, 2017.

About Martín Espada

Martín Espada was born in Brooklyn, New York, in 1957. He has published more than twenty books as a poet, editor, essayist and translator. His books of poems from W. W. Norton include *Vivas to Those Who Have Failed* (2016), *The Trouble Ball* (2011), *The Republic of Poetry* (2006), *Alabanza* (2003), *A Mayan Astronomer in Hell's Kitchen* (2000), *Imagine the Angels of Bread* (1996), and *City of Coughing and Dead Radiators* (1993). He is also the editor of *What Saves Us: Poems of Empathy and Outrage in the Age of Trump* (2019). His many honors include the Ruth Lilly Poetry Prize, the Shelley Memorial Award, the Robert Creeley Award, the National Hispanic Cultural Center Literary Award, an American Book Award, an Academy of American Poets Fellowship, the PEN/Revson Fellowship and a Guggenheim Fellowship. *The Republic of Poetry* was a finalist for the Pulitzer Prize. His book of essays and poems, *Zapata's Disciple* (1998), was banned in Tucson as part of the Mexican-American Studies Program outlawed by the state of Arizona. A former tenant lawyer in Greater Boston, Espada is a professor of English at the University of Massachusetts Amherst.